TERRARIUMS

Bring nature into your home

21 MINI-
LANDSCAPES
TO CREATE

MATHILDE LELIÈVRE

Photographs by
GUILLAUME CZERW

GINGKO PRESS

Mathilde Lelièvre
Garden designer

I was brought up in Brittany, in north-west France, and as a child I loved walking along the beaches or helping my grandparents on their allotment. No doubt it was these early influences that gave me a passion for nature and for gardening. So it was quite "natural" for me to study landscape gardening, with the intention of one day turning my passion into a way of life. In 2014 I set up my own business, Succulente Design Végétal, with the aim of helping people—especially people living in cities—to get back to nature.

Through this book and my work I hope to show that it's possible for everyone to live in harmony with nature, even if they don't think they have a green thumb or much time to spare.

Part decoration, part garden, terrariums are in fact one of the best ways to enjoy a little bit of the natural world every day—without even leaving home. All you have to do is understand a few basic principles, follow a few simple steps, use a little imagination, and … voilà!

CONTENTS

While vivariums (from the Latin *vivere*, meaning "live") are designed to house live animals and aquariums (*aqua*, water) are for fish, terrariums (*terra*, earth) are plant houses, gardens under glass. Each one is a miniature ecosystem, a tiny landscape that can be anything you want—woodland, desert, jungle, rainforest—based on the types of plant you choose to grow and the shape of the container you use.

Terrariums were all the rage in the 1970s, but the first one was created over a hundred years earlier, when an English doctor named Nathaniel Ward sealed a cocoon in a glass jar with some moist earth to observe the emerging butterfly and was surprised to discover, a few days later, that a fern and some grass had started growing inside it. The result was the "Wardian case," a kind of portable greenhouse that enabled plant-hunters to transport plants across the world and led to a revolution in agriculture and botany.

The cases were also adapted for domestic use to display tropical plants and became a popular feature of elegant homes in the Victorian era.

Today, as more and more people live in urban areas, with less and less contact with nature, terrariums are a clever and convenient way of bringing the natural world into our homes, where the often excessively dry air makes it difficult to keep certain types of plants and to enjoy nature on a daily basis. Each one is a uniquely decorative landscape, a self-contained ecosystem that requires little maintenance and is ideal for those who might not have a green thumb but nevertheless want to have plants growing inside their homes. And creating a terrarium can be fun—for both children and adults.

This book will tell you how to create your own terrarium, using different techniques based on the type of container and landscape you choose (closed or open, humid or dry …), and how to look after it.

A terrarium replicates the natural environment in which your chosen plants normally flourish. Choosing the appropriate container and the right type of substrate and soil are the keys to creating the terrarium you want—as well as keeping it at the right temperature and giving it the right amount of light.

Materials

Before starting to create your terrarium, make sure you have everything you need for each stage of the process. Then let yourself be inspired by the ideas presented here—which are only suggestions—to create the design you want. Making a terrarium is an art as well as a science, so feel free to express yourself!

DRAINAGE

Drainage is the first and most important consideration when making a terrarium, because glass containers have no holes at the bottom to allow excess water to drain away. So you must install a "drainage layer" to prevent the water you add (sparingly!) from soaking the roots of your plants and eventually causing them to rot.

01. Volcanic rock

Volcanic rock is a porous substance created by cooling lava. As well as retaining water and spreading it throughout the plant beds, it makes an attractive base for your terrarium. Pictured opposite is pouzzolane from the Massif Central in France, but other volcanic rock like pumice or perlite will work, too.

Alternatively …

You can also use clay balls, fine or medium gravel, or small stones to create your drainage layer.

DECONTAMINATION

Decontamination means keeping your terrarium healthy by preventing the build-up of mold, fungi, and unpleasant odors.

02. (Activated) charcoal

Activated charcoal (charcoal that has been treated with oxygen) absorbs certain toxins and reduces odors. Sprinkling some onto your drainage layer will help keep your terrarium contamination-free. You can buy it in garden centers or, if you have a fireplace, simply crush the burned wood.

But don't use barbecue charcoal, which is usually treated and can harm your plants.

SUBSTRATE

Substrate is essentially what your plants grow on. It can contain soil, clay, sand, peat, compost, and other "ingredients." You can buy substrate from garden centers or make your own, but make sure it's suitable for the particular plants you want to grow—whether leafy, succulent, epiphytic ("air plants"), bonsai, etc. It can be helpful to spray the substrate with water before planting. This will get the water circulating and help your plants to "take."

03. Leafy plants

For leafy plants (other than bonsai trees), your substrate should be light and free-draining so that it holds just enough water but allows any excess to drain away.

04. Bonsai trees

Bonsai trees have particular needs when it comes to both nutrients and drainage. Your substrate needs to be rich but open-textured to give them the best chance of flourishing.

05. Succulents and cacti

Succulents and cacti like dry conditions, so your substrate should include sand and be very free-draining.

06. Sphagnum

Commonly known as peat moss, sphagnum is a mossy material that can hold large amounts of water. It is particularly good for growing orchids and carnivorous plants.

DECORATION

A layer of sand, gravel, pebbles, slate, or various types of stones will not only further improve the drainage of your terrarium, but also add shape, texture, and color, and it will give your creation that final touch of imagination. You can find suitable materials in the aquatic plants section of your local garden center.

07. Large stones

08. Lichen growing on wood or bark

09. Flat white or grey pebbles (1–3 inch diameter)

10. White gravel (½ inch diameter)

11. Colored gravel (½ inch diameter)

12. Colored sand

13. Colored gravel (⅛ inch diameter)

14. Colored pebbles

Tools

You'll find suitable tools in your local garden center or pet store.
Some you'll have already or can make yourself.

• Wooden **sticks** with rounded ends to press the substrate into awkward corners. You can use large knitting needles or attach pieces of cork to smooth sticks or chopsticks.

• A **spoon** to help you place sand and gravel precisely where you want it.

• **Bonsai scissors** if you're planning to grow bonsai trees.

• A **syringe** to enable you to water only specific plants—or you can use a spoon.

• A **spray bottle** to create a fine mist that will add just enough water to keep your terrarium moist.

• **Brushes and micro-fiber cloths** to remove any dust or other residue from the glass and the plants themselves and keep them looking good.

What to do, step by step

If you follow these simple steps—with a little patience and creativity—
you'll have your very own terrarium in no time!

)1

After washing and drying your container, lay your drainage layer and sprinkle activated carbon over it.

)2

Use gravel or sand to make a decorative border around the sides of the container. Pick it up and turn it around to see what it looks like until you achieve the desired effect. This will give your terrarium interest and individuality.

)3

Then add the substrate you've prepared for your chosen plants. Use a spoon or a funnel if it helps. Press the substrate down lightly.

)3
cont.

If you're using sphagnum (for orchids or carnivorous plants, for example), soak it first in a bowl of water until it has absorbed as much as it will hold. Then squeeze it so that it isn't dripping and place it on top of the drainage layer. Before adding your plants, be sure to remove any soil or other material from their roots.

05 Make a hollow in the substrate large enough to accommodate the roots, insert these, and cover them with substrate, taking care not to bury the stem of the plant.

04 Carefully remove each plant from its pot and gently free the roots, so that these can establish themselves in the substrate in your terrarium.

TIPS : Avoid planting close to the sides of your container, as condensation on the glass could damage your plants. Try also to arrange them so that there is some space between them. If you include too many plants, they won't have room to breathe or grow.

06 Press down the substrate around the plant until it will stand by itself.

07 If appropriate (and depending on the type of plants you've chosen), you can add some moss to your composition. If it's dry, soak it in warm water for 15 minutes or until it has turned green, squeeze it gently and then spread it on top of the substrate.

08

Add your pebbles, gravel, or sand, using a spoon, if necessary. Use your imagination to re-create in miniature the landscape of your dreams!

09

Add a minimum of water to your terrarium according to the instructions for the type of plant(s) you've chosen, using a syringe or a spoon or your spray bottle.
When it comes to watering, *less is more*! It's easy to add water if you haven't watered enough, but not so easy to remove it if you've over-watered—which can be fatal to your plants. So go easy!

Once your plants have settled in and are starting to grow (unless they're bonsai trees, of course), don't be afraid to "trim" them by pinching off the ends of the longer shoots with your thumb and forefinger. Just by doing this, you'll encourage the plants to develop flower buds and new shoots near the base.

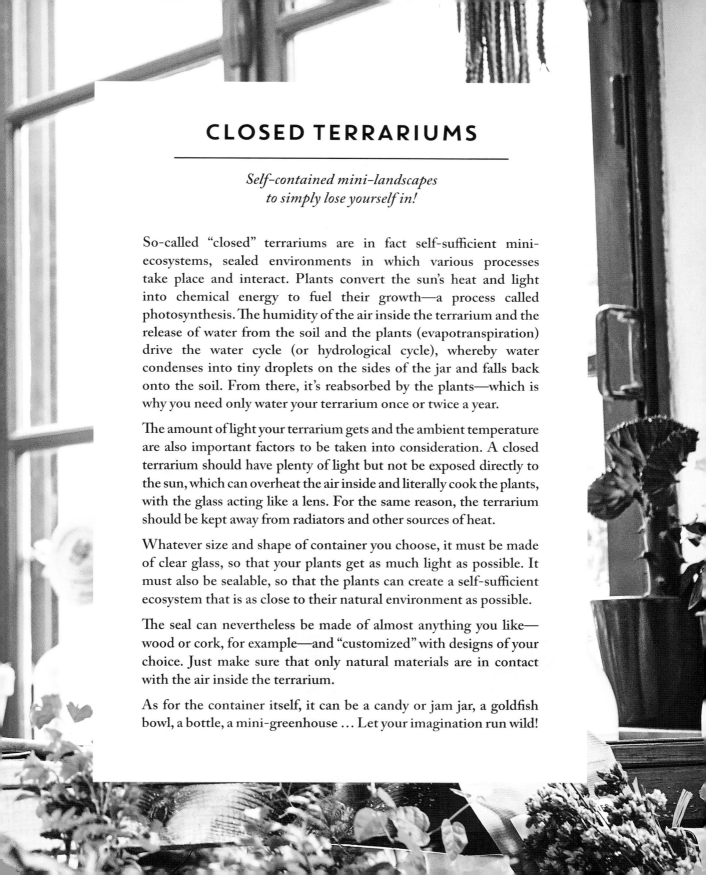

CLOSED TERRARIUMS

*Self-contained mini-landscapes
to simply lose yourself in!*

So-called "closed" terrariums are in fact self-sufficient mini-ecosystems, sealed environments in which various processes take place and interact. Plants convert the sun's heat and light into chemical energy to fuel their growth—a process called photosynthesis. The humidity of the air inside the terrarium and the release of water from the soil and the plants (evapotranspiration) drive the water cycle (or hydrological cycle), whereby water condenses into tiny droplets on the sides of the jar and falls back onto the soil. From there, it's reabsorbed by the plants—which is why you need only water your terrarium once or twice a year.

The amount of light your terrarium gets and the ambient temperature are also important factors to be taken into consideration. A closed terrarium should have plenty of light but not be exposed directly to the sun, which can overheat the air inside and literally cook the plants, with the glass acting like a lens. For the same reason, the terrarium should be kept away from radiators and other sources of heat.

Whatever size and shape of container you choose, it must be made of clear glass, so that your plants get as much light as possible. It must also be sealable, so that the plants can create a self-sufficient ecosystem that is as close to their natural environment as possible.

The seal can nevertheless be made of almost anything you like—wood or cork, for example—and "customized" with designs of your choice. Just make sure that only natural materials are in contact with the air inside the terrarium.

As for the container itself, it can be a candy or jam jar, a goldfish bowl, a bottle, a mini-greenhouse … Let your imagination run wild!

Care

Closed terrariums require very little care.

As well as regularly checking the humidity level inside your terrarium and watering it once or twice a year, be sure to remove any damaged, blackened, or fallen leaves, which will decompose very quickly in the damp atmosphere, possibly causing mold to form.

You should also trim your plants as soon as they touch the glass or start to "take over." Simply pinch off leaves and shoots with your thumb and forefinger or, for bonsai trees, use special scissors. After trimming, leave the terrarium open for 48 hours to let the plants "heal."

WHAT SHOULD I DO IF MY PLANTS' LEAVES TURN YELLOW OR FALL OFF?

If your plants lose leaves or their leaves turn yellow, this is usually a sign that there's either too much water or not enough inside the terrarium. If there's too much, leave the lid off for a while until the excess water has evaporated; if there's not enough, add water to the mosses and spray the whole landscape.

Yellow leaves can also indicate a lack of light. Check that your terrarium is getting enough light, and move it if necessary.

Brown marks on leaves are often caused by a fungus. Remove the affected leaves and leave the terrarium open for 48 hours so that any excess water can evaporate.

WHAT SHOULD I DO IF MOSS TURNS YELLOW?

If your mosses have dried out, soak them as suggested on p. 17 ("What to do, step by step," section 9). As they take up water, they should turn green again. If they don't, it's possible that they've been scorched by the sun or attacked by a fungus. Either way, you should replace them with fresh mosses.

WHAT SHOULD I DO IF MOLD APPEARS?

Mold is a sign that the humidity inside your terrarium is too high. Remove any elements that have mold on them and leave the lid off for 48 hours to let fresh air in and to stabilize the humidity level. After that, make sure you remove the lid whenever there's too much condensation inside the terrarium.

WHAT SHOULD I DO IF INSECTS GET INTO MY TERRARIUM?

A terrarium is a living thing, so it's quite possible that insects will make their home inside it.

If you notice small worms in the substrate, you can let them be; they won't do any harm.

However, if you see any mealybugs—which will look like a mass of feathery white blobs—or gnats or aphids start appearing, you should spray them with the appropriate product, being sure to follow the instructions carefully.

If you need to trim a bonsai tree, you should use special bonsai scissors.

Condensation

Terrariums are both self-sufficient and environmentally friendly because they recycle water.

That's why it's important to establish the right level of humidity and to check it regularly. This will create a balanced ecosystem and ensure that your terrarium stays healthy. Adding just enough water—a small amount only once or twice a year so that the substrate isn't soaked and the roots don't rot—should therefore be one of your prime concerns.

Tiny droplets and a light misting on the stopper and the sides of the terrarium are signs that the humidity is just right. However, if there are large drops of water and so much condensation that you can hardly see inside, you should open the terrarium and let fresh air in until the excess water has evaporated. Too much humidity for too long can cause a build-up of mold and unbalance the entire ecosystem.

On the other hand, if moss starts drying out—i.e., is dry to the touch or turning brown—and the substrate turns pale, this means you need to add water. But don't overdo it: a few spoonfuls will be enough.

When you've finished creating your terrarium and have given it an initial watering, leave it open for 24 hours so that any excess water can evaporate. During the first week, don't be afraid to leave the lid partially open from time to time so that the humidity in your terrarium can find its natural level.

PLANTS TO USE

The look of the plants you choose for your terrarium is very important.

Make sure your plants are healthy, compact, and vigorous. Avoid any with leaves that are dead or yellowing or have brown marks—or remove these if there are no others. Check that there are no insects on the underside of the leaves.

For a terrarium you need "miniature" plants—ones that have been cultivated specially so that they remain small—in pots no larger than 2½ inches in diameter. This is very important, since small roots will limit the plants' growth and allow you to create a more varied and interesting ecosystem rather than allowing your landscape to be overrun by fast-growing plants.

If possible, however, choose one more substantial plant (a bonsai tree, a fern, or a coffee plant, for example) that will give height to your composition (or possibly two, if you're using a large container). Also have low-growing plants to create an underlayer of different colors, such as *Fittonia verschaffeltii* or *Hypoestes phyllostachya*, and some climbing or trailing plants such as *Ficus pumila* or ivy, as well as mosses and other ground cover plants.

Before planting them, arrange your plants on a table or bench to get an idea of how they will look when they're inside the container.

All the plants suggested for closed terrariums come from tropical climates and flourish in a humid environment, so they will respond well to the conditions inside the container and feel completely at home as part of your terrarium.

01

Leucobryum glaucum -
Pincushion moss &
Bryophyta - **Small mosses**

GROUND COVER
& LOWER LAYER
(01–07)

03

Ficus pumila -
Creeping or climbing fig
(there are variegated varieties)

02

Hedera helix - **Trailing ivy**
(there are several varieties, with more
or less serrated leaves, and you might
prefer a variegated variety)

07

Soleirolia soleirolii
Mind-your-own-business

05

Hypoestes
phyllostachya
Polka dot plant

04

Fittonia verschaffeltii
Nerve or mosaic plant

06

Sagina procumbens
Pearlwort

10

Pellaea rotundifolia
Button fern

09

Asparagus sprengeri
Sprenger's asparagus fern

08

Coffea arabica
Coffee plant

11

Polystichum tsus–simense
Korean rock fern

UPPER LAYER
& BONSAI TREES
(08–16)

12

Nephrolepis cordifolia 'Duffii'
Lemon button fern

15

Polyscias filicifolia
Fern-leaf aralia or angelica

13

Nephrolepis exaltata
Sword fern

Ficus ginseng/retusa
or *Ficus microcarpa*
14 | **Bonsai**

Begonia rex
16 | **Painted-leaf begonia**

COOL ON THE HILL

A tree crowns the hilltop, its outline silhouetted against the sky. Surrounded by shrubs and garlanded with creepers, it watches over the valley below where, night and day, villagers go about their business.

)1 Line the bottom of a candy jar with volcanic rock a little less than an inch deep and place a lump of charcoal near the center.

)2 Pour in your substrate to make another 1-inch layer (or slightly more), pressing it down as you do so. Keep some to add later if necessary.

)3 Make a large hollow in the center and plant your bonsai tree. Scrape substrate from the sides of the jar into the hollow and firm it around the tree to make it stable and create a little hill.

)4 Using your wooden sticks, arrange the rest of the plants and decorative elements around it, alternating moss and small stones between the creeper, ivy, fig, and ferns to create contrast.

)5 Using a spoon or syringe, add a quarter of a glass of water to the substrate. Then spray the whole landscape. Leave the jar open for 24 hours to allow any excess water to evaporate before sealing it.

Make your landscape personal to you. If you want cleaner lines, put more moss and stones around the bonsai tree …

CARE)))))

CREATION)))))

COST)))

CONTAINER

• Candy jar
Diam. 7 in. (19 cm)
Height 9 in. (23 cm)

MATERIAL

• 3–5 handfuls of volcanic rock
• 1 lump of charcoal
• 6–10 handfuls of indoor plant compost
• Small stones

PLANTS

• *Ficus ginseng* bonsai
• Pincushion moss
• Creeping fig
• Trailing ivy
• Ferns

HIGH AND MIGHTY

CONTAINER

• Candy jar
Diam. 10 in. (25 cm)
Height 15 in. (40 cm)

MATERIALS

• 8–10 handfuls
of volcanic rock
• 1 lump
of charcoal
• Gray, black, and
white sand
• Gray and white
gravel (½ in. diam.)
• Gray and black
gravel (⅛ in. diam.)
• 15–20 handfuls
of bonsai compost
• Large stones

PLANTS

• Japanese pepper
bonsai tree with
twisted trunk
• Pincushion moss
• *Nephrolepis*
• Nerve/mosaic plant
• Creeping fig
• Trailing ivy

Soaring above a simple green landscape, the curved trunk of a majestic tree throws twisted shadows that mark out the passing of time as the sun slips silently across the sky.

〉1 Line the bottom of a candy jar with volcanic rock a little less than an inch deep and place a lump of charcoal near the center.

〉2 Make separate or mixed layers of colored sand and gravel around the edges to create the effect of rock strata.

〉3 Pour in a 2-inch layer of special bonsai substrate, pressing it down as you do so. Keep some to add later if necessary.

〉4 Make a large hollow in the center and drop in your bonsai tree, making sure to remove any soil from its roots first. Cover the roots with substrate and press it down firmly so that the tree stands upright.

〉5 With the help of your wooden sticks, add the decorative elements: the large stones to give structure, and the moss, fern, nerve plant, creeping fig, and ivy (as required to create the effect you want).

〉6 Using a spoon or syringe, add half a glass of water to the substrate. Then spray the whole landscape.

Your tree should be trimmed once or twice a year, or whenever the leaves reach the sides of the jar. After trimming, leave the terrarium open for 48 hours to allow the branches to heal. Then check that the tree has enough water before sealing the jar again. You can plant a different type of tree if you prefer, such as Ficus retusa.

JUNGLE IN A JAR

The cork stopper on this funnel-shaped jar keeps the lid on a tiny jungle bursting with spreading ferns and creeper-clad branches.

)1 Line the bottom of your container with volcanic rock just under an inch deep and place a lump of charcoal near the center.

)2 Pour in your substrate to make another layer just over 1-inch deep, pressing it down as you do so. Keep some to add later if necessary.

)3 Position the large stones first, with the help of your wooden sticks. Then add the planting, starting with the largest items: the ferns (Korean rock fern and *nephrolepis*). Finally, fill the spaces with the rest of the plants, the wood, and the mosses.

)4 Using a spoon or syringe, add half a glass of water to the substrate. Then spray the whole landscape.

Personalize your landscape by varying your choice of ferns—all of which will thrive in this humid environment—and by using different colored hypoestes.

CARE)))))
CREATION)))))
COST)))

CONTAINER

- Candy jar
Diam. 12 in. (30 cm)
Height 13 in. (32 cm)

MATERIALS

- 8–10 handfuls of volcanic rock
- 1 lump of charcoal
- 15–20 handfuls of interior plant compost
- Large stones
- Branches and bark covered with lichen

PLANTS

- Korean rock fern
- Blue star fern
- *Nephrolepis*
- Polka dot plant
- Variegated creeping fig
- Variegated trailing ivy
- Pincushion and small mosses

RAINBOW

Plants can be even more eccentric than people in their choice of "clothing," putting on all the colors of the rainbow: red, yellow, orange, violet, as well as green. Have fun creating a living firework display that will brighten any day.

01 Line the bottom of a candy jar with volcanic rock a little less than an inch deep and place a lump of charcoal near the center.

02 Make separate or mixed layers of colored gravel that will look like rock strata.

03 Pour in your substrate to make another 1-inch layer (or slightly more), pressing it down as you do so. Keep some to add later if necessary.

04 Add your plants, starting with the largest ones. Then complete the composition, complementing your color scheme with mosses and colored stones.

05 Using a spoon or syringe, add a quarter of a glass of water to the substrate. Then spray the whole landscape.

When planting, take care not to let too many leaves touch the sides of the jar, as the condensation could make them turn black and soon disturb the entire ecosystem.

CARE))))

CREATION)))))

COST)))

CONTAINER

- Candy jar
Diam. 9 in. (23 cm)
Height 11 in. (28 cm)

MATERIALS

- 2–4 handfuls of volcanic rock
- 1 lump of charcoal
- Colored gravel (½ in. diam.)
- Colored gravel (⅛ in. diam.)
- 5–8 handfuls of indoor plant compost

PLANTS

- Sprenger's asparagus
- Painted-leaf begonia
- Pink polka dot plant
- Creeping fig
- Trailing ivy
- Pincushion and small mosses

POP-UP PARK

This terrarium is a little world full of surprises. Behind every bush and tree lurk creatures just waiting to be discovered or to frolic across the fields. One of them might even be human ...

)1 Line the bottom of the jar with volcanic rock a little under an inch deep and place a lump of charcoal near the center.

)2 Make separate or mixed layers of colored sand or gravel around the sides to create an effect of rock strata.

)3 Pour in your substrate to make another layer just over an inch deep, leaving part of it unplanted.

)4 Position the coffee plant at the highest point, then the pearl-wort, and arrange the moss around to make little hills. Cover the unplanted area with pebbles and colored gravel to look like paths or play areas, and add your figurines.

)5 Using a spoon or syringe, add a quarter of a glass of water to the substrate. Then spray the whole landscape.

If you feel like it, move your figurines around or change them every so often so that your little park is always full of life!

CARE   ))))
CREATION   ))))
COST   )))

CONTAINER

• Candy jar
Diam. 6 in. (15 cm)
Ht. 7½ in. (19 cm)

MATERIALS

• 2–4 handfuls of volcanic rock
• 1 lump of charcoal
• Natural and black gravel (⅛ in. diam.)
• 5–8 handfuls of indoor plant compost
• Flat white pebbles (1–2½ in. diam.)
• Natural, gray, and white pebbles (½ in. diam.)
• Figurines

PLANTS

• Coffee plant
• Pearlwort
• Pincushion moss

BOX OF DELIGHTS

CONTAINERS

• Dish
Diam. 7½ in. (20 cm)
Ht. 2½ in. (6.5 cm)
• Cloche
Diam. 9 in. (23.5 cm)
Ht. 15 in. (39 cm)

MATERIALS

• 4–6 handfuls
of volcanic rock
• 1 lump of
charcoal
• Natural gravel
(⅛ in. diam.)
• 8–12 handfuls
of bonsai compost
• Large stones

PLANTS

• *Ficus* bonsai
• Pincushion moss
• Creeping fig
• Trailing ivy

Like a treasured antique in a glass bell jar, this terrarium is a real Pandora's box of unexpected objects: coins, medals, relics, bones, works of art … A mysterious and wonderful landscape that is limited only by your imagination!

)1 Line the bottom of the jar with volcanic rock a little less than an inch deep and place a lump of charcoal near the center.

)2 Make separate or mixed layers of colored gravel around the sides to create an effect of rock strata.

)3 Pour in a 2-inch layer (or slightly less) of special bonsai compost, pressing it down as you do so. Keep some to add later if necessary.

)4 Make a large hollow in the center, right down to the drainage layer, and plant your bonsai tree, making sure to remove any soil from its roots first. Cover the roots with compost and press it down firmly so that the tree stands upright.

)5 Using your wooden sticks, add the rest of the planting and decoration to make a satisfying composition. Start with the larger stones to create structure; then fill in with the moss and creepers.

)6 Using a spoon or syringe, add half a glass of water to the compost. Then spray the whole landscape. Replace the bell jar to seal the terrarium.

Place the container in a well lit position but not in direct sunlight. If it's against a wall, turn it periodically so that all the plants get the same amount of light and grow at the same rate.

WASTE NOT, WANT NOT

The great thing about terrariums is that you can create them in almost any clear glass container that comes your way. So have fun transforming ordinary storage jars, old vases, unused cafetieres, empty bottles, and flasks—and anything else you can find—into eye-catching mini-landscapes!

)1 Line the bottom of your container with volcanic rock a little less than half an inch deep. Then build up successive layers of sand and gravel until the whole drainage layer is just over 1 inch deep.

)2 Place a lump of charcoal near the center and pour in your substrate to a depth of just under 1 inch, pressing it down as you do so.

)3 Using your wooden sticks, plant your plants right in the center, and then arrange the moss and sand around them.

)4 Using a syringe, add a soup spoonful of water to the substrate. Then spray the whole landscape.

This is the perfect terrarium for children to make! Make sure they have lots of different-colored sand and plants, and they'll soon have their hands covered in earth!

CARE ❭ ❭ ❭ ❭
CREATION ❭ ❭ ❭ ❭
COST ❭ ❭ ❭

CONTAINER

- Preserve jar
  Diam. 4 in. (10 cm)
  Height 7 in. (18 cm)

MATERIALS

- 1 handful of volcanic rock
- Colored gravel (⅛ in. diam.)
- Colored sand
- 1 lump of charcoal
- 1–3 handfuls of indoor plant compost

PLANTS

- Creeping fig
- Trailing ivy
- Nerve/mosair plant
- Pincushion moss

POWER HITTER

With a large wooden ball balanced on top, this terrarium is a guaranteed home run. The Polyscias *perched on a rocky cliff is enough to make anyone dizzy with excitement!*

CARE ⟩⟩⟩⟩⟩

CREATION ⟩⟩⟩⟩⟩

COST ⟩⟩⟩

CONTAINERS

- Vase
Diam. 7½ in. (19 cm)
Height 14 in. (36 cm)
- Wooden ball
Diam. 4½ in. (12 cm)

MATERIALS

- 3–5 handfuls
of volcanic rock
- 1 lump of
charcoal
- Gray gravel
(½ in. diam.)
- Gray and black
gravel (⅛ in. diam.)
- Gray sand
- 6–10 handfuls
of indoor plant
compost
- Large and medium-
sized stones

PLANTS

- Polyscias
- Creeping fig
- Variegated
trailing ivy
- Pincushion moss

01 Line the bottom of your vase with volcanic rock a little less than an inch deep, and place a lump of charcoal near the center.

02 Make layers of sand and gravel to look like rock strata.

03 Pour in the substrate and build it up in the center so that it's 2 inches deep there and just a quarter of an inch at the sides. Press it down lightly.

04 Plant your tree at the highest point, surrounding it with the large stones to create the effect of a clifftop.

05 Use the smaller stones to stabilize the construction and, between them, plant the creeping fig and ivy. The moss and sand should add the finishing touch to your escarpment.

06 Using a spoon or syringe, add a quarter of a glass of water to the substrate. Then spray the whole landscape.

You can also get creative with the stoppers on your terrariums! Choose from cork, wood, or resin, and paint or decorate them to complement your design.

LES ESCALES

KAREN VIGGERS
roman

LA MAISON
DES HAUTES
FALAISES

Open **TERRARIUMS**

OPEN TERRARIUMS

Delightful little deserts!

So-called "dry" or "open" terrariums are ideal environments for cacti and succulents, which thrive in a dry atmosphere. With a large opening at the top, they allow air to circulate inside and create a microclimate that's perfect for plants whose natural habitat is desert or semidesert and grow in dry, sandy soil.

The word "succulent" refers to plants that have thick, fleshy leaves, stems, or roots for storing water—which means that cacti are a type of succulent.

Hardy, easy to look after, and amazingly varied, succulents make vibrant and often surprising terrariums.

When it comes to containers, anything goes! Fish tanks, bowls, vases, dishes, jars, lampshades … almost anything as long as it's glass. The choice is yours!

Care

Listen up—your succulents will tell you what they need …

You create an open terrarium in the same way as a closed terrarium (see "What to do—step by step" on pp. 15–17), using a substrate suitable for succulents. How you look after an open terrarium, however, is quite different, since there's no water cycle to maintain.

But, with the exception of *Tillandsias*, succulents require very little water and can survive long periods of drought, which makes them very easy to keep. Water them once every 10–15 days, making sure the substrate has completely dried out each time, and they'll be quite happy.

You should give each plant a soup spoonful of water, around the base. Be careful not to leave any water lying on the leaves, as this can damage them.

Succulents have an annual "cycle" that you should follow by reducing your watering between October and February, when they are dormant. A little water once a month will be enough.

Finally, ensure that an open terrarium is in a well lit position but not in direct sunlight, since the container can act as a lens and burn your plants.

WHAT SHOULD I DO IF THE LOWER LEAVES DRY OUT AND FALL OFF?

Don't worry; this is part of the plant's natural biological cycle. The lower leaves die off and new ones grow out from the center of the plant. Simply remove any dead leaves from your terrarium.

WHAT SHOULD I DO IF THE LEAVES WRINKLE OR WILT?

This means your plants are thirsty! Wrinkling or wilting are signs that a succulent has almost used up its reserves of water. Give it some water and … problem solved.

WHAT SHOULD I DO IF THE LEAVES OR STEMS LOSE COLOR?

It's likely that your plants aren't getting enough light. Try moving them to a brighter position.

WHAT SHOULD I DO IF THE BASE OF THE PLANT GOES LIMP?

This means you've given it too much water! If it isn't completely limp, let the substrate dry out totally before watering it again. If it's too far gone, remove it immediately from the terrarium to prevent the build-up of mold and replace it.

Use a soup spoon to water your succulents.

PLANTS TO USE

*Check that your plants are really healthy
before you put them in your terrarium.*

Just like leafy plants, succulents must be in good condition: no brown marks, limp or damaged stems, or drooping leaves. Check them also for insects.

When it comes to succulents, you're spoiled for choice. There are thousands of different varieties, in all shapes and sizes and with various textures and colors of leaves. But you can rest assured that they're all just as simple to look after.

Depending on the size of your container, you may be able to combine larger and smaller plants. Succulents grow very slowly, so your design will retain its shape, without any plant "taking over."

Finally, remember that humidity is the succulent's worst enemy, so don't use any mosses in an open terrarium. However, you can exploit the textures and colors of stones, gravel, and sand to your heart's content!

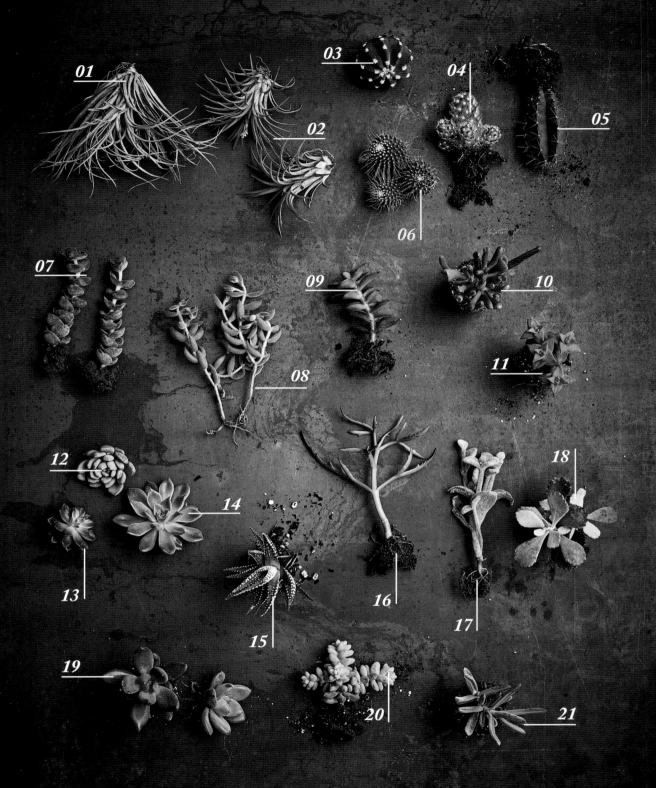

01

Tillandsia ionantha
"Silver"

03
Small cactus

04 | **Small cactus**

05
Small cactus

EPIPHYTES
(01–02)

02
Tillandsia ionantha
"Rosea"

CACTI
(03–06)

06 | **Small cacti**

07
Crassula
"Bride's Bouquet"

09
Crassula ovata
Jade plant

10
Crassula ovata
"Hobbit"

11
Crassula perforata

08
Crassula
mesembryanthemoides

12
Small hybrid
Echeveria

OTHER SUCCULENTS
(07–21)

18 |
Kalanchoe pumila

14
Large hybrid
Echeveria

Kalanchoe
"Green Spider"

13 | **Small hybrid**
Echeveria

16 |

17 | *Kalanchoe eriophylla*

15 | *Haworthia*
fasciata

19
Pachyphytum

Sedum burrito
20 | **Donkey's tail**

21

Senecio serpens
Blue chalksticks

FLOATING ON AIR

Epiphytes are plants that grow on other vegetable matter and so don't need planting in any kind of substrate. They're simple to look after, too, so creating a stunning terrarium with epiphytes is as easy as falling off a log!

)1 Spray your plants with mineral water without letting any get inside them. Then hang them upside down to dry.

)2 Line the bottom of your vase with stones, pebbles, gravel, and sand to create whatever colorful patterns you choose.

)3 Push the branches covered with lichen gently into this base so that they stand upright.

)4 Place your *Tillandsia ionantha* "Silver" on the base material, without "planting" it, and then wedge the *Tillandsia ionantha* "Rosea" in the branches.

Every 2–3 days (every 10 days in winter), remove the plants from the terrarium and spray them with water. Allow them to dry before replacing them.

CARE)))))
CREATION)))))
COST))

CONTAINER

• Vase
Diam. 6 in. (15 cm)
Height 14 in. (35 cm)

MATERIALS

• 6–8 handfuls of gray and white gravel (½ in. diam.)
• Black, gray, and white gravel (⅛ in. diam.)
• Black and white sand
• Flat gray and white pebbles (1–3 in. diam.)
• Branches and bark covered in lichen

PLANTS

• 1 *Tillandsia ionantha* "Silver"
• 3 *Tillandsia ionantha* "Rosea"

TREASURE TROVE

CONTAINER

- Glass display case
  with metal edges
  Height 12 in. (30 cm)
  Width 7 in. (17.5 cm)
  Depth 7 in. (17.5 cm)

MATERIALS

- 4–6 handfuls
  of volcanic rock
- 1 lump of
  charcoal
- Small gold and
  yellow stones
  (⅛ in. diam.)
- Gold and yellow
  sand
- 8–12 handfuls
  of cacti compost

PLANTS

- 5 assorted small
  cacti
- *Crassula* "Bride's
  Bouquet"

This terrarium is like a pirates' chest with its lid half-open, revealing a treasure trove of tiny cacti. But don't let anyone try to grab it; this bullion is only for looking at!

❯1   Line the bottom of the box with volcanic rock a little less than an inch deep Then add the charcoal, the little stones, sand, and compost—either in layers or mixed together—to a total depth of 2½–3 inches.

❯2   Plant your cacti and *crassula* (wearing gloves) and press the substrate down around them with your wooden sticks to make sure they're firmly anchored.

❯3   Then sprinkle some more sand and stones around the plants.

❯4   Using a syringe, add a small amount of water to the ensemble—no more than a teaspoonful per plant.

Cacti are averse to humidy, which makes them rot, so wait until the substrate is completely dry before you water them again—and never water too much. In winter, your cacti will be dormant, so give them hardly any water. And remember always to leave the container partly open.

EMERALD ISLE

This terrarium is like an island floating in the center of your table, where succulents of all shapes and shades rub shoulders in an elegant glass bowl.

)1 Line the bottom of the bowl with volcanic rock a little less than an inch deep and place a lump of charcoal in the center.

)2 Pour in the substrate to a depth of a little over an inch and press it down lightly.

)3 Plant your succulents, starting with the largest and, with the help of your wooden sticks, filling the spaces with the smaller plants and the stones.

)4 With a syringe, give each plant a soup spoonful of water at its base.

When you water your succulents, take care not to allow any water to settle on the leaves, which can damage them. Wait until the substrate is completely dry before watering again.

CARE)))))
CREATION)))))
COST)))

CONTAINER

• Bowl
Diam. 10 in. (25 cm)
Height 4 in. (10 cm)

MATERIALS

• 4–6 handfuls of volcanic rock
• 1 lump of charcoal
• 8–12 handfuls of cacti and succulent compost
• Small stones

PLANTS

• *Kalanchoe* "Green Spider"
• Jade plant (*Crassula ovata*)
• *Crassula perforata*
• *Haworthia fasciata*
• *Echeveria* hybrids

MINI-TERRARIUMS

You can make as many of these tiny terrariums as you like, using brightly colored sand to brighten up a table or decorate a shelf. Mini-terrariums can enliven even the smallest spaces!

CARE 〉〉〉〉〉
CREATION 〉〉〉〉〉
COST 〉〉〉

CONTAINERS

• Dishes
Diam. 3 in. (8 cm)
Height 2 in. (6 cm)

MATERIALS

• 1 handful of
  volcanic rock
• Colored sand
• Colored gravel
  (½ in. diam.)
• Colored gravel
  (⅛ in. diam.)
• 1 lump of
  charcoal
• 1–3 handfuls
  of cacti and
  succulent compost

PLANTS

• Large and small
  Echeveria hybrids
• *Crassula perforata*
• Donkey's tail

)1 Line the bottom of each small bowl with volcanic rock. Then add sand, gravel, and small pebbles in layers until you have a drainage layer just over 1 inch deep.

)2 Put a lump of charcoal in the center and then pour in the substrate to a depth of just under an inch, pressing it down lightly.

)3 Plant your cacti and succulents using wooden sticks.

)4 With a syringe, give each plant a soup spoonful of water around its base.

Rather than throw away small glass jam or yoghurt jars, use them to make mini-terrariums. You might want to tie a colored ribbon around them to add to the effect.

SNOW GLOBE

Succulents come in a wide variety of colors, which allows you to create landscapes of subtly contrasting shades. Here, plants with frosted leaves turn your terrarium into a cool winter scene.

)1   Make a 1-inch layer of white stones at the bottom of your bowl and place a lump of charcoal in the center.

)2   Pour in the substrate, alternating it with layers of smaller stones and sand to make another 1-inch layer, pressing it down gently.

)3   Plant your succulents, starting with the larger ones. Then add more stones and sand to heighten the frosty effect.

)4   With a syringe, give each plant a soup spoonful of water around its base.

You can create quite a different landscape using shades of pink, green, or yellow.

CARE)))))
CREATION)))))
COST)))

CONTAINER

- Small goldfish bowl with a wooden stand
Diam. 5 in. (12 cm)
Height 7 in. (17 cm)

MATERIALS

- 3–5 handfuls of white gravel (½ in. diam.)
- 1 lump of charcoal
- Gray and white gravel (⅛ in. diam.)
- Gray and white sand
- 6–10 handfuls of cacti and succulent compost

PLANTS

- Blue chalksticks (*Senecio serpens*)
- *Kalanchoe eriophylla*
- *Kalanchoe pumila*
- *Pachyphytum*
- *Echeveria* hybrids

GREEN DIAMOND

CARE))))))

CREATION))))))

COST))))

CONTAINER

- Diamond-shaped
  container with metal
  edges
  Height 8 in. (20 cm)
  Sides 6 in. (15 cm)

MATERIALS

- 1–3 handfuls
  of copper-colored
  gravel (⅛ in. diam.)
- Copper-colored sand
- 1 lump of
  charcoal
- 3–5 handfuls of
  cacti and succulent
  compost

PLANTS

- *Crassula
  mesembryanthemoides*
- *Crassula ovata*
  "Hobbit"
- *Haworthia fasciata*
- *Echeveria* hybrids

A little gem of a terrarium, housing desert-loving succulents that look stunning from all angles. Whether suspended or standing on a table, this multi-faceted display will always attract attention—without demanding too much of it from you!

)1 Line the bottom of the container with gravel and sand to a depth of just over 1 inch.

)2 Place a lump of charcoal in the center and pour in the sustrate to a depth of just under an inch, pressing it down gently.

)3 Plant your succulents using wooden sticks.

)4 With a syringe, give each plant a soup spoonful of water around its base.

You can use cacti or epiphytes instead of these succulents for an equally brilliant effect!

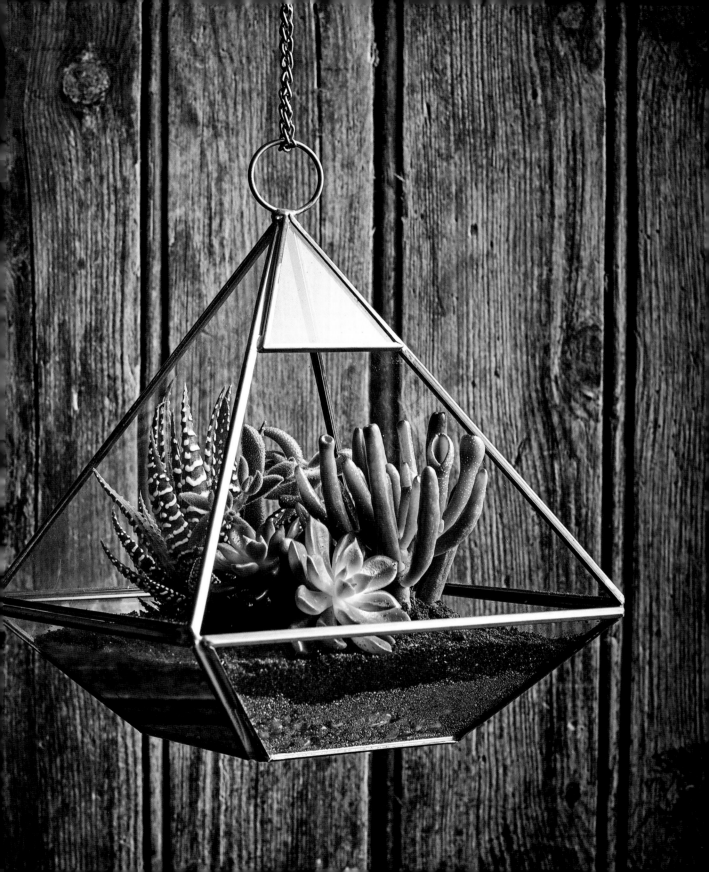

LOW PROFILE

This shallow vase will be most effective at eye level, on a shelf, against a wall, where you can observe your changing desert landscape as if through a porthole.

)1 Make a 1-inch layer of large white stones at the bottom of the vase and place a lump of charcoal in the center.

)2 Add layers of smaller stones and sand, plus the substrate, until these are just over an inch deep, pressing them down gently as you do so.

)3 Plant your cacti an inch or so apart and fill the gaps with stones to create a desert-like effect.

)4 With your syringe add a teaspoonful of water to the base of each plant.

Instead of cacti, you can use other succulents or epiphytes, such as Crassula mesembryanthemoides *or* Crassula *"Bride's Bouquet." As this terrarium will be seen from the side, make sure the layers of substrate are sharply contrasting!*

CARE ⟩⟩⟩⟩
CREATION ⟩⟩⟩⟩
COST ⟩⟩⟩

CONTAINER

• Shallow fishbowl
Diam. 11 in. (28 cm)
Height 8 in. (20 cm)

MATERIALS

• 3–5 handfuls of white gravel (½ in. diam.)
• 1 lump of charcoal
• Natural, gray, and white gravel (⅛ in. diam.)
• White sand
• 6–10 handfuls of cacti and succulent compost
• Small stones

PLANTS

• 5 assorted small cacti

EXOTIC TERRARIUMS

The terrariums described in this section don't fit the categories of "closed" or "open" terrariums and require special techniques or maintenance—whether because of the type of container or the type of plants inside it. Some feature leafy plants in an open container, which need careful management and regular watering; others have flowering plants, whose leaves must be trimmed to encourage them to bloom; and then there are the carnivorous plants, which need a particular type of substrate …

However, even these terrariums are quite simple to create—and they give you the opportunity to experiment with different techniques and explore an almost infinite variety of effects.

PLANTS
TO USE

*For these terrariums you can use all kinds of
plants, as long as you ensure they have the
right environment in which to flourish.
In fact, the sky is the limit!*

Phalaenopsis
Moth orchid

01

Asparagus plumosus
Climbing asparagus

02

03

Adiantum cuneatum
Delta maidenhair fern

04 | *Peperomia rotundifolia*
Trailing jade

05 | *Peperomia* "**Pepperspot**"
"**Pepperspot**" peperomia

06

Oxalis regnellii
Shamrock plant

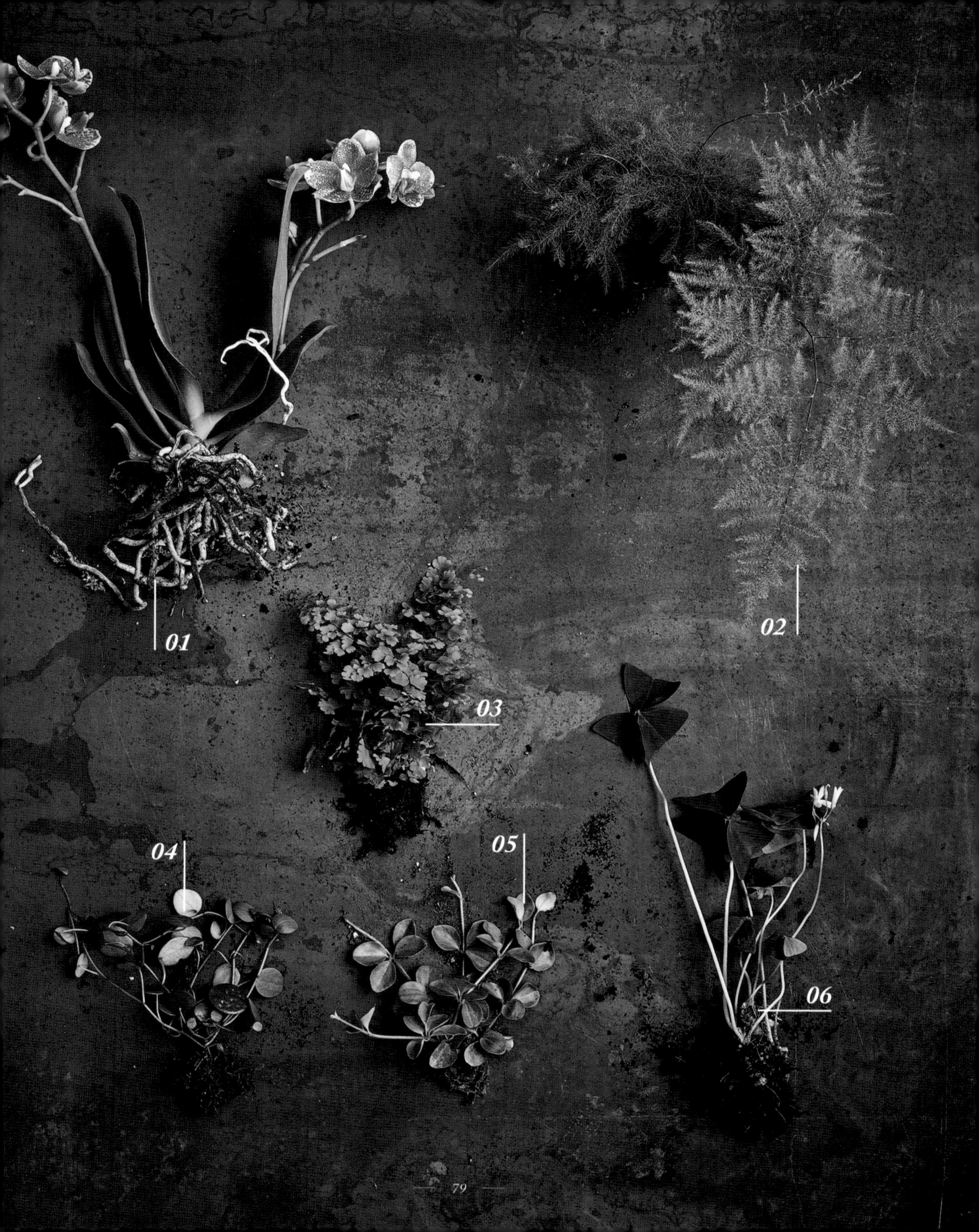
01
02
03
04
05
06

MAN-EATER

Observe these curious creatures of the plant world at your leisure through the glass of your terrarium. Carnivorous plants live by catching and ingesting insects. Strangely fascinating, they nevertheless have specific requirements, which you must be sure to meet ...

CARE   〉〉〉〉〉

CREATION   〉〉〉〉〉

COST   〉〉〉

CONTAINER

• Rounded vase
Diam. 8 in. (20 cm)
Height 22 in. (56 cm)

MATERIALS

• 3–5 handfuls
of volcanic rock
• 1 lump of
charcoal
• 6–10 handfuls of
hydrated sphagnum

PLANT

• Sarracenia

)1 Line the bottom of the vase with a layer of volcanic rock just over an inch deep and place a lump of charcoal in the center.

)2 Soak the sphagnum and add a 2-inch layer on top of the volcanic rock.

)3 Remove your carnivorous plant from its pot and "plant" it carefully in the sphagnum, pressing this gently around its roots to hold it in place.

)4 Using your syringe, give the plant half a glass of distilled (demineralized) water and then spray the whole composition liberally—also with distilled (demineralized) water. The water must be demineralized because carnivorous plants are used to very poor soil and cannot assimilate minerals.

Carnivorous plants love humidity, so don't be afraid to spray them (with distilled/demineralized water) every day. You should also check regularly that the sphagnum is good and moist. Make sure the terrarium is in a light position, but not in direct sunlight. And if a leaf turns brown, don't worry; simply remove it from the container.

INTO THE WOODS

Lose yourself in a mass of ferns and mosses as you explore this woodland scene delicately shaded by a towering asparagus plant.

CARE 〉〉〉〉
CREATION 〉〉〉〉〉
COST 〉〉〉

CONTAINER

• Large fishbowl Diam. 16 in. (40 cm)

MATERIALS

• 8–10 handfuls of volcanic rock
• 1 lump of charcoal
• 15–20 handfuls of indoor plant compost
• Large and small stones

PLANTS

• Climbing asparagus
• Pincushion and small mosses
• Creeping fig
• Trailing ivy

〉1 Make a 1-inch layer of volcanic rock at the bottom of your bowl and place a lump of charcoal in the center.

〉2 Pour in the substrate, heaping it 2 inches deep in the center and pressing it down gently. Keep some to add later if necessary.

〉3 Make a large hollow in the center and plant the climbing asparagus, after removing any soil from its roots. Then cover these with substrate, pressing it down firmly so that the plant stands by itself.

〉4 Use your wooden sticks to complete the composition: place the large stones first to give it structure; then fill the gaps with mosses, creeping fig, and ivy until it looks the way you imagined it.

〉5 Using a syringe or spoon, add half a glass of water to the substrate and then spray the whole landscape.

This terrarium is left open, so there is no water cycle as there is in closed terrariums. Therefore, you must keep an eye on humidity levels and regularly add water. Water the plants once a week and spray the whole arrangement daily. If the mosses dry out, remove them and soak them in water until they regain their color (see step 7 on p. 16).

FLOWER POWER

CARE)))))

CREATION)))))

COST)))

CONTAINER

• Vase
Diam. 10 in. (24 cm)
Height 14 in. (36 cm)

MATERIALS

• 6–8 handfuls
of volcanic rock
• 1 lump of
charcoal
• Hydrated sphagnum
• 10–15 handfuls
of indoor plant
compost
• Wood and bark
covered with lichen
• Small stones

PLANTS

• Orchid
• Korean rock fern
• Mind-your-own-
business
• Creeping fig
• Pincushion and
small mosses

An orchid emerges mysteriously from a carpet of moss and ferns in this dense sub-tropical forest landscape. Its brilliant flowers are like a burst of sunshine and will take your breath away every time you look at them.

01 Line the bottom of the vase with a 1-inch layer of volcanic rock and place a lump of charcoal in the center.

02 Remove your orchid from its pot, wrap its roots in moist sphagnum, and place it in the center of the terrarium.

03 Pour the compost around the sphagnum, pressing it down gently to stabilize the orchid.

04 Plant the Korean rock fern, mind-your-own-business, creeping fig, and other creepers, interspersing them with moss, wood, bark, and small stones.

05 With a syringe, add half a glass of water to the substrate and then spray the whole arrangement.

Orchids, mosses, and ferns love humidity, so be sure to keep levels up by spraying your terrarium regularly. Give the plants a little water once a week, too.

LIGHT FANTASTIC

Imagine an old lantern, lying abandoned in a shed, that has been invaded by ivy, moss, and creepers—a natural takeover that results in a luminous little landscape ... You can create this very effect as easily as lighting a candle!

)1 Line the bottom of the lantern with a 1-inch layer of volcanic rock, ensuring that none will fall out when the door is open. Then place a lump of charcoal in the center.

)2 Pour in the compost and make it slope upward away from the door to a depth of 2 inches, pressing it down gently as you do so.

)3 Plant your ferns, starting at the highest point. Then arrange the moss and mind-your-own-business in clumps. Use the stones to make the composition look natural and unplanned.

)4 Using a syringe, add half a glass of water to the compost. Then spray the whole landscape.

Make sure your landscape is constantly humid by spraying it daily and watering the plants every 10 days.

CARE))))
CREATION))))
COST))

CONTAINER

• Lantern
Diam. 6 in. (15 cm)
Height 10 in. (24 cm)

MATERIALS

• 3–5 handfuls of volcanic rock
• 1 lump of charcoal
• 6–10 handfuls of indoor plant compost
• Small stones

PLANTS

• Delta maidenhair fern
• Pincushion moss
• Mind-your-own-business

HANGING GARDENS

CONTAINER

• Suspended bowl
  Diam. 8 in. (20 cm)

MATERIALS

• 3–5 handfuls
  of volcanic rock
• 1 lump of
  charcoal
• 6–10 handfuls
  of cacti and
  succulent compost

PLANTS

• "Pepperspot"
  peperomias
• Trailing jade

Terrariums don't have to be standing on tables or shelves; they can just as easily hang from the ceiling or from a beam or bar to make a leafy canopy over your living space. You can even suspend terrariums of different shapes and sizes at different heights to create your very own hanging gardens!

〉1 Line the bottom of your bowl with a 1-inch layer of volcanic rock. Then place a lump of charcoal in the center.

〉2 Pour in compost until it's about 2 inches deep, pressing it down gently.

〉3 Plant your peperomias, starting at the back and alternating "Pepperspot" with trailing jade. Plant the one with the longest branches last, letting them tumble out of the opening.

〉4 Using your syringe, add half a glass of water to the compost. Wait until this has dried out completely before watering again.

Originally from South America, peperomia is a family of plants with highly decorative leaves. There are over 1,000 species of peperomia, so feel free to explore them to find the colors and shapes you like best.

LUCKY CHARM

With its clump of shamrock plants, this terrarium should bring you luck, while its elongated shape makes it seem like the cross-section of a landscape—a soil sample inviting analysis. Either way, you can give free rein to your imagination in creating it.

)1 Line the bottom of the container with the coarse gravel, then add the sand and fine gravel in uneven layers until you have a rocky foundation up to an inch deep.

)2 Grind up a piece of charcoal and sprinkle it over the drainage layer. Then pour in the compost, again in varying thicknesses, to complete your "slice of countryside."

)3 Use wooden sticks to plant the shamrock plants, pressing the compost around them.

)4 Arrange the mosses, alternating bushy and flat plants, and add the pebbles to make a stronger outline.

)5 With a syringe, give each plant a soup spoonful of water.

Oxalis is a perennial and forms bulbs or rhizomes. There are many different species, offering a variety of leaf shapes, colors, and flowers for you to explore.

CARE))))
CREATION)))
COST)

CONTAINER
• Rectangular vase
Width 4 in. (10 cm)
Depth 2 in. (5 cm)
Height 6 in. (15 cm)

MATERIALS
• 3–5 handfuls of white gravel (½ in.)
• White sand
• White gravel (⅛ in. diam.)
• 1 lump of charcoal
• 6–10 handfuls of indoor plant compost
• Flat white pebbles (1–2½ in. diam.)

PLANTS
• Shamrock plant
• Pincushion and small mosses

Sources

*You should easily be able to find everything you need
to make your terrariums in local or nationwide stores.
Here are a few suggested sources:*

GLASS CONTAINERS

Suitable containers can often be found in
stores selling kitchen storage jars and bottles
(for cookies, candy, preserves, pasta …)
or home décor (vases, bowls, jugs …).

Glass containers of all kinds and to suit every pocket can be found at nationwide home décor stores such as At Home, IKEA, and The Container Store.
Find exciting new uses for them!

Online shoppers should check out:
save-on-crafts.com
couronneco.com
....

For cork stoppers try:
Jelinek Cork Group (jelinek.com)

But by far the best source of unusual
containers is yard sales, garage sales,
and flea markets!

PLANTS AND OTHER MATERIALS

Most garden centers and nurseries
will be able to supply you with volcanic rock, charcoal,
different types of compost, mosses, and, of course,
all the plants mentioned in this book.
For the more adventurous among you,
I suggest browsing the catalogs of specialist
horticultural suppliers.

Everything you need for your terrarium
can be found at:
Terrain (shopterrain.com)
terrariumusa.com
twigterrariums.com
....
For plants suitable for most terrariums, try:
glasshouseworks.com
neherpetoculture.com
....
For a range of succulents, check out:
mountaincrestgardens.com
simplysucculents.com

Don't forget to look around you and pick up anything
that might be useful from the countryside, roadside, or seaside …
You might be surprised by what you can find!

ACKNOWLEDGMENTS

First of all, I would like to thank my parents and my brother, who always supported me while I was researching and writing this book, as well as the rest of my family and my friends for their unfailing support. I must also thank everyone I've met through Succulente Design Végétal, who have enabled me to turn my passion for plants into a daily pleasure. Finally, a big thank-you to the whole team that put this book together and helped me through the process of writing it.

Succulente

•

Design Végétal

http://www.succulentedesignvegetal.com/

Published in 2018 by:
Gingko Press Inc.
1321 5th Street
Berkeley, CA 94710, USA
www.gingkopress.com
ISBN 978-1-58423-713-6

Translation from the French:
Joseph Laredo © **Gingko Press Inc.**
Typesetting: **Weiß-Freiburg GmbH**
Printed in Spain by **Grafica Estella.**
Published originally under the title:
Terrariums
© **2017 by Éditions Solar,**
Department of Place des Éditeurs, Paris
English translation copyright:
© **2018 Gingko Press Inc.**

For the original French edition:
Director: **Jean-Louis Hocq**
Editorial Director: **Corinne Cesano**
Editors: **Anne Kalicky, Comptoir**
Éditorial
Editorial Collaboration: **Mathilde Poncet**
Copy-Editing: **Clémentine Sanchez**
Design: **Le Bureau des Affaires**
Graphiques
Fabrication: **Laurence Duboscq**
Reproduction: **APS**